Attributed

to the

Harrow

Painter

KUHL
HOUSE
POETS

edited by

Mark Levine and

Emily Wilson

Attributed
to the
Harrow
Painter

Nick Twemlow

....

....

University
of Iowa Press
Iowa City

University of Iowa Press, Iowa City 52242
Copyright © 2017 by Nick Twemlow
www.uipress.uiowa.edu
Printed in the United States of America

Design by Omega Clay

The University of Iowa Press is a member of Green
Press Initiative and is committed to preserving natural
resources.

Printed on acid-free paper

Library of Congress Cataloging-in-Publication Data
Names: Twemlow, Nick, author.
Title: Attributed to the harrow painter / Nick Twemlow.
Description: Iowa City : University of Iowa Press,
[2017] | Series: Kuhl House poets
Identifiers: LCCN 2017005981 | ISBN 978-1-60938-541-5
(pbk) | ISBN 978-1-60938-542-2 (ebk)
Classification: LCC PS3620.W46 A6 20107 | DDC 811/.6—
dc23
LC record available at https://lccn.loc.gov/2017005981

Contents

*This book
is for
my son,
Sacha
Sebastian
Wolf*

Attributed

to the

Harrow

Painter

Looking at Schnabel's *The Death of Fashion*
with my son

As we stood
In the unreflective
Pall of the canvas
Neatly pocked by broken
Plates, light
Swallowed by
The sickly sweet strokes
Of crap paint
Clumsily
Slapped across it,
I picked up Sacha
& asked him
If it might be
A bit much,
The painting's title? but
He already had designs
On the Brancusi
He had glimpsed
In the Des Moines Art Center
Catalogue, which he then pawed
On the floor of the
Entrance room—
So plush were the couches
I fell asleep
Reclining into one.
Woke in a fright,
Turned off the lights!
Walked into a courtyard
Terrifically cold—the water-

······ 1

Fall tending my dreams
Froze midstream,
Reflecting brilliant
Fresnel light!
The artist
I follow from year
To year, sometimes
Years pass
But I find him
Launching another
Lantern down the river
Frozen to river-
Bottom
& so I
Whispered into
Sacha's delicate
Ear—are we able
To meet these
Monuments *as is*?
What if, say, you had happened
Upon a David Salle painting
(Rarer these days)?
What if your stepmother
Was in the same art class
In high school as Salle,
Doodled the same
Inane nothing-of-notes,
Desperate for a way
Out, not just of this class
But of this gap
Between herself &
What she might

Want to become.
David Salle, don't
Sweat the small
Devils detailing
Your
Lamborghini Countach
(Sounds so garish,
To talk this way
About the '80s, I mean
That model was like
The Ford Escort
Of the Jet Set)
& then David Salle
Went on to snort
The entire decade
Into his rectum. She
Demurred
Rightly, the pain
Ticked into my
Stepmother &
Soon enough her spine
Began off-gassing
A barbiturate haze
Five miles in every
Direction.
This feeling we all
Know each other
From some past life
Spent holding hands
Walking over the precipice
Into the volcanic bowels
Of Hell, this otherness,

Fixed into a buried
Set of neurons native
To homo sapiens sapiens,
Has surfaced surfaced
With a fury,
Furious with spouts
Of pepper spray
Spraying
The frozen air
Waiting for history's
Next victim to occupy,
Occupies the space
In front of it.
The snow,
I wrote,
To paraphrase
Myself, to interpret or
Delay
My words, to rework,
Remix, mash up,
Redefine, defile,
Lift, smash, plagiarize,
Borrow, beg, steal,
Augment, as homage I
Distill my words
Into a bitter rye,
Drink it to bottoms
Up!
I looked out,
I had my protagonist
Look out a wintry
Window, each snowflake

Like a soldier whipping
A horse yoked
To a chariot,
This Greece,
This Rome,
This vatic
Impulse to stay
Connected swirling
All round, said
In passing,
My soul swooned
Slowly
As I heard
The snow
Falling faintly,
Through
The universe
& faintly falling,
Like the descent
Of its last end.
So you
Tell me
How your
Radical formalism
Saves lives
Exactly?
What I've got on view
Out my office window
Is luxurious paradisiacal
Snow stirring in me
A soul-destroying
Desire to snort some

Adderall,
After all.
This could be your
Legacy, Sacha,
This art
You have been
Forced to feed on
For eons.
             I
             Sink into the
             Couch in my office,
             Fall asleep
             Watching *Stalker*,
             Slowly fall
             To the bottom
             Of the never-ending
             Well,
             This tonic
             Murmur—
             Something about making
             Sure all the locks were
             Locked.
             I don't know
If I checked them.
So I check them
Repeatedly.
This bedroom farce
A ray of sun
Fazing across
The televised haze
Of some future
My son takes out

A second, maybe
Third mortgage on,
He plugs into the din—
His cryo-mortal coil.
I can't wait
Until he goes loco
Slurping snow cones,
Lisps with the asps
In ancient Egypt.
The overdub
Is imperfect, a few frames
Late, so when
Sacha looks at
"The Death of Fashion"
Hanging against this
Well-lit wall &
Says, "This looks like
Garbage," the only word
That matches his mouth
Is the end of everything.
No one goes out
Like this

The speaker's feeling of loneliness is profound,
or I read the lyrics of the emergency

When I picked up my son
From preschool this
Moment willed itself
Into being
& nuffingness, like when
I tethered myself
To his teacher.
We lifted off
To the clouds,
Such happy balloons!
Her smile a ridiculous
Rainbow that streaked
Across my sightlines.
There was the climbing
Structure Sacha fell from
& bit off
His tongue. There was
Nothing to be done.
His face bled
& his face bled.
All the new finking
Is about floss.
In this it resembles
A ham sandwich.
Sunday morning
Watching Sacha
Put a puzzle together
Is like sitting shiva
For the family addict

Who tapped every
Vein. I don't
Know where to fix
My eyes. Sunlight
Sticks to the blinds
Like germs
To a lung, love to the gun
That hovers in front
Of each step I take
To the bathroom,
The bedroom, the office
Counter where
I register
Sacha's documents
& stamp him into
Oblivion. I'm not sure
How much more melancholy
I can take from this life.
In the terrible light of the moon,
Under the crush
Of the news
They brought—
What kind of list do you require?
Desire? What do you need
To be reminded of your
Obsolescence? I can
Go on, but do you need
Me to?
I read the lyrics of the emergency
As they ticked across his eyes.
Little man I said as I
Gripped his shoulders

Let me call you
Wolf.
These lyrics offer nothing.
Stolen & begged for,
They relieve
No one as they relive
The traumas
That deploy from this gangrenous
Architecture of my past,
Which I've grafted
Onto you.
Forgive me.
I mean this.
I can't help but
Write about you, so
Forgive me all these years
In advance. I'm an addict.
You can easily redact it.
By the time you're old enough
To read this you'll be old enough
To erase.
So, this is how my recent
Parent-teacher conference
Went down, a few weeks
Before you turned four,
Ate a peach cupcake,
& told me you'd like
To be an Astronaut Artist
Who eats glass & shoots up
Silvered strains of the
Human experience
When you're galactic &

Needle-happy.
Good for you! My praised
Genius, you have lofty goals!
& don't worry so much
About whether they think
You're a boy or a girl.
You have much
To look forward to
In the matrix
Of gods & trends.
Years ago, I started
Saving everything for you

  Me: What do you do all day?

  Wolf: I self-select. I sort things.

  I pour water from one cup into another.

  Me: What is your rapport

  With your classmates?

  Wolf: I am a respectful watcher.

  I am an observational learner.

  I can smell their weakness.

  I study them. I hone in . . .

  Me: He appears to be coming unhinged.

  Teacher: He's calm in class. A real

  Leader. Children follow him. He

  Has so much to say, so many ideas—

For the lyrics of emergency
I need an
Interpretation engine
To drive you
Into my eye
Which refracts
Terrible moonlight the cost

Of choosing to atomize
These days—
O wolf of memory! Medallion
Of the meanest arts!
Son, you won't remember
Any of this so drive
Into tomorrow as if
You have nothing
To gain nothing
To peruse.
I'll be thinking of you
Armed with your vicious
Youth
Your tabula rasa affect
Your deep understanding of nothing
      Wolf: Why do you challenge me?
      Me: What do you mean?
      Wolf: I wasn't talking to you.

Mothland

All along you were Right, they were Flanking our
house They Documented you taking off Your clothes
every morning I requested these Documents & they
sent someone's Illicit hard drive I fucked with the
commandant Nothing that mattered Continued to
happen into the Nothing that made us laugh like Gas
does Most of us went WYSIWYG Which meant sand
kicked In our face &/or our Life was a fracking disgrace
I know you lived mostly Desirous of desolation A
kind of Interior branding a Lesbos of the Soul Let me
introduce you To my friends Who fry bacon & Spumoni
de Kooning cooling limbic An astral fryer Thomas
Mann Spelling out things I exhausted I falling down
On my face the divorce Anything but legal Just shame
& egrets Shitting the windows I realm I record Life
begins to get in The way the life Of a novelist Which
I assume is not Only more comfortable The advance
is ridiculous But strident The perqs develop Their
own antiquities I always go back to my Preference
for medications that act swiftly I don't do time-lapse
So well I get hell I focus my gaze On Takashi Ito's
Structured vision Of the not this world But space is the
place Where we can mace the strangers walking into
our loathsome Into oblivion The usual I refuse My son
Wallows the smooth Tallows of the luxurious paradise
of Time to spinneret to Pearl the moustache I get that
You falsify Perfectly you stream experience Like a coin
you toss Into whatever Fountain I still Believe the
poem Delivers a brutal shrill lust for streaming Cusps

your romance With écriture If my mother were To read this How much shame Would envelop Her I'm Sure you assure us Reassured all of us Which might mean Write out & out & out else Make this a god Or homeless People to shine a light On a poem amending The title Intended to circumscribe My mother's loneliness I am thinking of My mother a lot These days which Pass in spasms In theory If we are anything If we have nothing else uncommon My mother Finds comfort in Planting bulbs each fall She left me a voicemail Message for my birthday Several days late to which I never responded I didn't Listen to it for months I can't remember If I did listen to it Fred told me he couldn't Get over a line from the Poem I read in Chicago This summer from a poem that shows up later in this book

"Look, I've loved my mother Most of my life."

Its permission to admit why the anxiety Over mother love Why depict spiders skittering All over our dreams I didn't mean I didn't always Love my mother her Name is Robyn same As my wife When Oedipus says *I get The feeling* His dumb Luck is his fortune Is his *is* Oedipus Reminds us to behave Better in the future Which his motherwife Reminds us is unknowable Every memory I have Or choose to have Of my mother saturated In the blues of a Dusky sky I should Cry I should inhabit The clichés entrusted to me To exhibit A lonely boy ill Treated defeated before Birth exiled from Chance When I Remember my mother Crying I don't remember Her ever crying She loved me I'm certain As she loved her Spring tulips not unconditionally But with proper proportion Unhappy that I cannot heave My heart into my mouth I Love your majesty According to my Bond no more nor less the man standing Next to me inside of me in Permanent ecstasy the cyphers Scuttling under passing cars Unable to find A shadow to Dissolve Into The barrel Of a gun twists Back at me I lard The scene with A company of C's I see the scene in every Register but time-Lapse returns No favor The mother coma The mother comma The various strobing Or phasing The clock dial is a riot Planning itself Years in advance Go quietly address The vending machine Snip wires Stare at Pictures of you Jolted twenty feet back onto The hood Of a viper Flicking its Capital relentlessly At the brine of these new centuries Erupting like nothing You or I know I pick at a scab I develop A hankering for Insta for gratification A door that slides Shut just As invasion of talk Of jetties & molly & away To Somalia As if you could evade The glistening Of your Fund which powers up In a shadow Enciphered this cruel media this papering Over & proxy servers & Anonymous nerve Tapping to allocate resource Assuaging Assange Buffering Beyonce Journos Copping a feel In Ferguson ecstasy of Entering the Gilgamesh Dying 'neath the heath Hammered to a tinsel thin Instance of justice You don't belong To tribe always acting as Leering at The contents of the mirror Mirroring the Warhol Insistence on or the Basquiat Keith Haring! Nauman walks in a square that Occludes race & class Privilege preening or Peacocking Queer Theory rasterized Resisting salve of Semiotics Your brother arches His eyebrow Thought This true & u spend so much of

yourself Spending credit scores & fantasy The vale
we Vulture in our waking dread Waxing what You
examine with your niggling X-ray You my standing
Camino All the world's nostrils flare & Zenith & zeroes
shiver Me back into my car & I Drive home totally

Champagne Dawn

Cassandra wrote
To tell me
That my
"Problem
With chicks
Is over,"
& I jumped out of
My chair
& ran
To the picture
Window
In the living
Room,
Threw open
The curtains,
& saw
My neighbor
Hacking
His rake
At the still-
Fluttering
Body
Of a
Barred
Owl.

On a Clear Day

Just imagining
The inside
Of a triangle.
It feels like what
The fetus feels
Surrounding it as it
Accelerates into being.
If I can find each space
That constellates here,
I might stop shaking
My child long & late
Into the night
That is day that is
Night in this blight.
Who says that?
I do!
I do!
What about the moment
When you thought you heard
The midwife say
"Dead,"
The confusion
Fused us. I was supposed
To grab it & declare its
Sex—I had been preparing
For this
For weeks.
The midwife handed it to me
As she said "Dad,"—
It was my time to own

The moment
Like it was a sandbag & the
Great flood beckoned.
You heard her say "Dead."
A few seconds passed—
Extended into eternity—
& you emptied
Out of everything,
Let loose into a limbic abyss.
What is that space like?
Does it fit here? Is it a star
In this constellation?
Is it a space you can move
Through? Is there time?
These, are they
Moments of decision?
That seems
Wrong. I suspect
No thinking takes
Place *within* the triangle,
This enveloping space
In which utter crazy.
Where the degrees
Agree with me.
Or, rather, thinking may
Take place, but no action
Is made on these thoughts,
Beyond mere thinking.
Is this like drowning?
I haven't drowned.
Is this like waking
From a dream?

I haven't dreamed before.
Is this like the light at the end
Of the tunnel?
In this space,
Things cease to mean,
She writes. Things
Aren't even things,
She continues. The light
In here sickens me.
That's not what she said.
The poet, when ill,
When feverish, when aflame,
This is when she inhabits
The space. The moment
She looks at me with such
Pity. Do you hurt?
Always.
Do you want to
Continue?
Do you?
There it is, moving
Toward me.
The midwife says,
"Dad." She said it
With a certain expectation.
This was a game of
Transference & I realize
Now you were
Expecting something
From me—a simple thing.
Who is this creature?
I realize you heard her say

"Dead."
You think it's dead.
It was Sacha. I wept.
This is what I said to you:
"It's Sacha!"
There is
A moment when I
Believe everything
You are saying, but then
I look at you.
You still don't know
If he's alive, if he's *being*.
Some poet wrote about
This space, time out of,
That it was without
Horror but was
Terrifying.
But only—maybe it's you
Recalling in hindsight—
Did it *feel*
This way.
There wasn't even
A during.
To take this away
Would be to
Me, you wrote,
Nothing. If I see
A dark presence
Moving through
The ocean, I ask
Of it if it
Feels the water

Surrounding it,
Or if the sun—
You could type
That right onto
My lungs,
You whisper
The leaves to sleep,
You have this power,
He tells himself,
You breathe us
Into being.
Why, how does this
Happen, what
Is happening
Right now.
I look behind me
At the cord
As it lightly
Bounces off the window shade.
Your voice echoes
Laughter
Like light
It fills every space
It tilts its face . . .
I am because
Of you, you no longer
Write. Who is
This man
Recording
Me?
When I tell you
About my nightmare

In which you are,
What,
You just being you,
I am filled
With dread—
Whatever it is
The content has never
Mattered.
At your age
You should
Be, I don't know,
You write,
I don't know
What it means anymore
To be alive. When
He looked at me,
Before I said anything,
& I held him in my arms.

I wanted to write you a love poem

By the time I started writing,
I had just come in
From the back patio,
Where I had seen
The moon's reflection
In the water feature. I laughed
To myself, wondered
How the water caught
The moon, which seemed
Pitched at too queer
An angle. & what
Was being featured?
I once wrote,
"Nothing is too anything,"
I'm thinking tonight that
I'm right.
But I'm not sad.
Just saddened. I
Breathe. I circulate.
My body would like to tell you
How much it can't
Stand to tell you
What it wants to tell you.
Here's a sample: Teeth. Stomach.
Skin. Application.
Yard. Wood trim.
Gutters. Teeth
Teeth stomach teeth.
I spend all of my time
Creating novel ways

To distract myself
From the need to
Distract myself.
One minute goes like this:
You don't want to know.
That's the hardest part,
Conveying how just being
Just feels.
My latest concern
Is our son. Seeing him
Alone
Pinned against
The wall at Willowwind
By some apparitional collector
Of lost souls, the kid who
Was the first to locate an
Afterlife for Sacha. It sounded,
From his lips,
Like melodrama. We all see
Some kind of light & we
Tunnel toward it & how did this
Even happen? I wept
Later that night.
I know it's just a moment among
The millions, & there is
James & is he always
Thinking about.
Stereo-death, little Telemachus,
Defending a ghost most
Of his life, his mother
Obsessed with
Subtle refractions of light.

(She's a Rayist at heart).
I'm not saying you're
Unraveling a weave
Every night. I think
That's what I do
These evenings,
Typing pixels
Unto oblivion.
Sitting Lotus
On a massive lily pad
On a pond
Somewhere in fifth century
China.
Dentist. Acid reflux. Dentist.
Stillpoint . . .
I hold the chakra
Position as long
As possible.
I imagine
All my obsessions
Abstracting into a color,
Sometimes
A version of blue,
Sometimes
I can't work it out,
I have such
An impoverished
Color palette
To work with, so I get
Caught up
In this, my inability to see
Color in any interesting way,

& then
The whole thing falls
Apart & I am back
In here, where
The walls are pink
& the pixels
Laugh like dropsied clowns.
Some kind of plague
Takes hold.
Some kind of plague riots
In the grid I can't keep
Track my teeth need immediate
Attention do I look fat
In this shirt where
Is my focus? Stillpoint. Hellish
Laughter rings through my ears
Teeth, teeth, migraine,
A reprieve, I can
Go to sleep
For a moment once I
Stomach dentist root canal
Like the worst kind of comedy
You expect to laugh
But the laugh
Never comes.
As it were, the moon
Did that, this glint
Stomach still point do you
Love me Sacha do you
& will I ever be
More than the sum
Of my regressions

Which compile
Like maggots
Of data
Eating through
A server in Reston, Virginia
Where teeth annul &
Stomachs inhere
& I think I am inventing
In ultimate
Infinity
A category of
Sadness
As I punch
These keys
& I hope you have
A really
Wonderful reading

Burnett's Mound

There was a time
We parked your Cutlass
At Burnett's Mound
& lit fires across
Topeka's horizon,
Which was always
Flatlined. My father
Once played a recording
For me of a dude we sorta
Knew in high school, under
Hypnosis. He recalled
Being abducted here by aliens
While he was preparing
To make out with his gf.
Right where we had stood.
He sounded so high
On the recording
I recognized the sound
Of your voice. The traumas
He articulated paled
In comparison. When you point
To that gray swirl of smoke
At horizon's edge
Tell me
It's the spitting image
Of Aegipan wielding
An animal leg in
Titian's *Bacchus & Ariadne*
(All the action is on the right).
I spew out the hit I've just taken,

Cough-laughing until I see
Stars molesting each other
In my periphery.
No wait, that's the guy
Describing an amorphous
Mass of green goo
Pushing into his Camaro
Just as he's mounting
His gf. It absorbs him,
He tells his therapist,
Under the hood of hypnosis.
The first thing he thinks
Is this is how in utero felt?
Why am I not more scared?
He recalled his father
Picking him up
From school for lunch,
He was maybe seven, his day
Already lost to the nice
Weather beyond the windows,
& his father asked him
If he'd like to eat a stone.
Something
Is happening, he said he thought
To himself, as some kind of
Interstellar light pushed into
His anus. It was like a key.
He told them everything.
All the gum he stole from
His local grocer; watching
His mother weep
Into her vanity;

Later, walking Kira,
Justin, & Jenny
Through their first time
Dropping acid &
Translating what
The hyacinth was saying.
After the session, when
His therapist snapped
His fingers &
He was back
With the world,
He remembered
The expression
On his gf's face.
She didn't reach after
Him, she just smiled
& made sure he wasn't
Holding the keys.
O Andy,
Were all this true!
Is it lazy
To daydream
About our past
Like this, like it
Was a novel flush
With nuance & intricacy?
Look Andy, we shared
A few years of uncontrolled
Aggression & it's
Caught up to us.
I just want to know
What happened

To my mother
That day I walked into
A bar.
The bartender said,
Why the face.
I said to the bartender,
Let us spin gold from
Our tangled veins!
Rip them from our bodies
Like copper wire
From cheap drywall in
Apartments rotting
With black mold that lingers
Long after the flood waters
Recede back into the river
Womb! Doesn't that sound
Fun! Look,
I love the sound of
My own voice, you can ask
My wife, my friends,
My best enemies.
They'll nod in agreement
& please pass the mustard!
Just last week, right after
George at Buzz! cut my hair
Into a mess of bad decisions
(Just kidding, George, I practically
Died when I saw my hair
The next morning, after all
Your magic had evaporated),
I wrote a few emails, mostly
Responding to queries about

My son's preschool's sudden
Outbreak of head lice. I felt
Sick, like a dog tossing
His biscuits all over the proletariat
(I promised Žižek, who's on my
Speed dial, I'd nod in his direction
At least once in this poem!).
O Andy, what happened—
We used to talk, between
Bong hits, about everything
We thought worth
Talking about!
We didn't just live
In a bubble, we built
The fucker breath by breath.
Sometimes, it felt like
We lived in your Cutlass,
Cutting class to smoke
Some Lamb's Wool
In the parking lot
At the public library
& head in to figure out
What that self-proclaimed
Satanist who asked for a lighter
Had said about pig
Sacrifice.
We were students of something.
Complicit
As two plugs of dirt that comprised
The Great Unwashed. But
We don't need a revisionist
History to tell us all this,

Do we?
I'm just a dude fat & happy
Reminiscing, converting an all-male
Style—let's not kid ourselves,
Barbara Guest was hardly
A New York School poet,
Hard as her apologists
Try to winch her in—
She was so much more.
She had to be, & Ashbery's
Been so hard to dump on
These past few decades
I feel constipated right now.
You see what I did there?
I'm thinking of Lance & Jason
& Zach & Zoble &
Sometimes, I feel this nausea
I spoke of much earlier
That has me wondering
If all that playtime I sucked
Into my clean lungs when I was
Little makes any real sense
Now.
My father says some things
Over the phone
Tonight. He's so inexact
& clichéd in his thinking
I want to workshop everything
He's ever said to me. Because,
As you know, my mum
Prefers to plant bulbs this time
Of year. She once told me how

Awful her fingers felt after
A few hours digging. The room
Swelled into a hell I only
Imagine you wish you weren't
Familiar with. This vicious
Life coursing through you.
Like when we walk Michigan Ave.
Remember to tuck our
Wallets deep inside our tremulous
Veins. I swear, Andy, Fred,
My life was wasted
Years ago, when "I had nothing left to,"
Had lost all meaning.
I love you, Andy, Fred,
Like old souls who've
Finally returned to find
Nothing is what was promised.
Poetry is super duper,
In a loop, say it with me.
I'm fine with all this
Pretend stuff
About how my friends are
My only real audience
Except didn't some of us
At least have slightly bigger
Ambition? The heaviest word
I know, the one that haunts
Everyone listening, the reams
Of digital waste we've spent
Discussing it, debating it,
Posturing & this heavy
Petting via our many lists

& wasn't that dinner party
Simply fabulous, J.D. or
Louise or whomever you please.
It's the rain shadow behind
The ricin you've imagined
Carefully mixing into
The last bottle of red
At the party you spent
The bulk of on the balcony
Chain smoking, overhearing
The Gay '90s replay itself
All night like you knew
History was just a shell game,
Its hands appear to move
Too fast only if you take
Your eye off long enough.
How
My father's mother,
A Maori named Marion,
Was collected thus,
As many before & after her,
From her whanau
By well-meaning white
Reps of the Queen's
Colonialist Enterprise.
(The Queen I hate
Wasn't Queen yet but I hate
Her with all my being,
Her percussive silence,
Her contusive diamonds,
Her comforts. My mother
Spends retirement

Reading about her
As she tends to the dead
Among us.)
They had been dispatched
To erase the native tongue,
Replace it with a correction,
The language, which I employ now
To recall Marion listening
To in the ballads of Jim Reeves,
An American crooner,
Lesser known than his rival,
Buddy Holley. Both died in
Plane crashes, both spooned out
In sugary lines & Reeves sang her
Into a state of being
Happy to be alive & that's
What happens when
Resistance is not a futile
Gesture, but impossible,
& when a foreign tongue
Takes over & dumps
The fresh carcass of its
Capital all over your land.
In my poetry workshop today,
I challenged my students
To name five poets
Who didn't walk into a room
With a rant in their pants,
Hungry for something beyond
Their job description.
Do you remember, Andy,
That time my brother

Climbed the radio tower
On the isolate island
Next to his apartment,
Maybe one hundred feet, totally
Yet imperfectly high,
As we were, & all I kept
Saying to myself was,
What kind of story is he
Trying to become? This
Was one angry man,
White as dirty snow,
Raging against the frying light
With the speed of an avalanche
On a lonely mountain.
I anticipate
Everything that happened
Today a few weeks ago as
I typed this.
I continue to talk
About myself
As gnats assemble themselves
Against high contrast back-
Grounds just to get laid.
I should've never left
New York, but what choice
Did I have? The day
Robyn & I were thrust
Into an O. Henry story,
Taking different trains
To the same Italian place
In Soho to meet friends
For a dinner we'd agreed to

A while back & I slipped
Into a bar to nurse
A few fingers of shit whiskey
While considering
An offer to run a film magazine
That offered no health insurance
& promised that I'd
Be reminded daily
How terribly my film
Career was coming along
As I wrote forgettable
Paragraphs on the future
Of 16mm. Robyn
Sat across from me
Later that night in the
Space in our Greenpoint apt.
That passed for our
Kitchen, tapping her
Pointer finger in a
Metronomic lull
(She had to pry
My face from that table
So many times,
She's become expert
With a crowbar) &
This lull pulls
Nothing into focus:
She'd gotten a call
That day too,
Teaching gig in
Eugene, the name of
An old boyfriend

Of my mother's,
The one who sold
Toy trains to enthusiasts,
Armed with a rich absence
Of enthusiasm, he was
Counterweight to so much
Childishness in the adult world,
Policing the very idea of play
& he never once gave me
A thing.
We left New York,
& now, a decade later,
I realize this was our
Finest moment.
I can't keep up
With this speed, all the flaring
Nostrils the sadness
I feel every time I walk
Downtown with you, Fred,
As you point out the dis-
Crepancies in the grid.
There was a time when
I was rather attenuated
To all this business of being
Radical, regardless of what
It might mean to write
A good sentence. You just
Name names, make a name
For yourself. Most of the poets
I've met feel ashamed.
At the money roasting
In their savings accounts,

But why not release yourself
To a world that will rip you apart
Limb by fucking limb, blood
In blood out, let us badge
Our faces, our hands
With blood 'til blood
Everywhere a golden
Shower of blood!—
Be not ashamed of who
You aren't. Money is
For nothing. Practice,
If you feel shame,
The homeless smile:
It begs of you
It feels nothing
It ties into a knot
In the stomach
It is a blur,
From your distance,
A blot in the sky
Of an otherwise
Perfect day.
Writing at length may be
An act of resistance,
But this is no battle.
I left my axe to burn
In the bowels
Of the cave
I burned brightest in.
I wield a Taser
These days, shocking
The horizon so as

To fry open a seam.
I can see into my past. It is
Littered with Styrofoam
Teeth, a rather
Candid admission that talk
Isn't cheap, it's disposable.
Let me tell you
Andy, Fred, there was a dog
I nearly killed. I've told his story
A dozen times, maybe more,
& every time it ends
So bountifully! It is the parable
Of the good life, the one in which
We value life itself, hold it up
As our collective raison d'être.
Does it matter the details?
This dog was not a dog
But Cerberus himself!
His lust for life was legend.
Your past, he said to me,
Is of no interest. Your present
Induces a migraine.
Your future has me in stitches.
I know a good time, he continued,
I like a good laugh. As if
The lily's petals came to
Real human life. Andy,
We are never alone in that life
Because we have fertilized this one
With summary opinions.
Pace Lispector, "I'll miss
Myself so bad

When I die," the nautilus
Of light spirals shut,
The hem of your lips
Where is my son?
Supreme darkness.
The distant sound of coughing.
Cerberus exhausted, sickly
From his endless labor.
This brutal hunger,
Unrequited, hardened
Into stone calcified
By the endless wash
Of impure blood.
The blood of fools
Bled for our sins
In the language of signs,
A range of genuflection
Only God could decipher.
Then, the blue jay
Landed at my feet,
Shockingly blue
Wired into the moment
Because bird, because
All of this absurd.
When I can't find the right
Word, I blame it on the bird.
I woke up the next day
Awash in localized pain,
Little sleep, work ahead,
Already thinking toward
The end, when I can
Blot out the day with

Whatever's at hand.
To be a poet means to be
Quiet.
You walk
With a limp.
You seduce
Your students
With authority.
You wake up
Tomorrow unsure
Of things. It's that
Simple. You're unsure.
Imagine this fact:
You fucking woke up today!
So you type the unimaginables.
You dress up your life.
You wake up sometimes
Basking in a specific kind
Of morning glow & you
Set down words. You answer
Your emails, you brew
Another pot of coffee,
You cry. You try & you cry.
You wonder, What happened?
But look around! You have it all!
A roof over your head
Three squares. Clothes that
Fit, a Wi-Fi connection. Google
Alerts, so you can stay on top
Of. Your ears burn, it's your
Amazon ranking recalibrating.
You spike to 5,000

Then on to oblivion.
Andy, Fred, this is what
It means to be modern.
This kind of
Pathetic self-surveillance.
What do you know,
Cerberus, here's Shirley
Fucking MacLaine!
According to Charley Tart,
My dad's old friend from
The experiment of the '60s,
Whom I shared
Fried shark with one night
In the last attempt
At a restaurant in Topeka,
Where the closest a shark
Came was in my memory
Of Stellen dropping two
White tablets the size of my
Fist into his aboveground pool
To stabilize the chlorine levels
As he tells me—I'm three
At the time—that those
Tablets are about to turn
Into sharks with a single
Purpose in mind, & Charley
Tart, what do you know,
He sprinted through
Our conversation like
He had somewhere
Not better to be
But just to be

& since he coined the term
"Altered States,"
He had earned his
Local celebrity.
I remember
He just opened
His mouth:
"Shirley had just stopped
To give way to a passing
Comet when we pulled up
Behind her. She then tried
To move off but her
Core-essence stalled. I waited
Two nanoseconds
Then mind-honked her.
This she didn't appreciate,
Judging by the stream of
Expletives she telepathically
Bombarded us with.
Good heavens! The lady
Was not only out of her body,
She was also out of her mind!"
Feed her to the alligator
Of happiness. Let the ancient
Beast tear her to shreds!
Let us watch clips
Of Cerberus devouring
Her mind-honked spirit!
Fred, it's never a good idea
To just be yourself,
Let work roll off
The body like water.

My cousin Finn
Died two weeks
Ago. You would've liked him,
I'm guessing, but I'm guessing
Because I haven't talked
To him since 2005.
We can begin the process
Of brushing Hong Kong
From our shirt folds
As it flakes into our wonderful
Futureless past. Some kind
Remark he made on my elegance
Really stuck with me
& I'd like to think
Everything changed, but nothing
Ever really does. That's so tired
A position, his Mum grieves,
His sister disbelieves,
His father turns over in a box
Aflame in the Philippines.
All the world's ablaze right now.
It's been thirty years since he
Flew in & the life I had yet to live
Had yet to falsify
Continues to record.
All this data
Busting the seams.
There was his smile,
Etched into the mantle above
The fireplace, it talked
Me out of so many
Worries, but the worries

Always came back
With the speed & clarity
Of a wolf howling under
A harvest moon on a t-shirt
In a truck stop. Finn, who are you,
Anymore? Dust?
Your mother fetal on the floor
Next to your bed? Your sister
Tearing up her house
In search of anything
You might've touched.
How did you do it,
Isolate flower, this method
Of self-annihilation? I mean,
We all do it in some way.
I just brushed against a pedestrian
With my car he was plugged
Into his soundtrack
Walling him off
His phone throwing so many
Voices at once I felt nauseated
After he walked off the curb
Into my path I didn't
So much brush against him
As smashed him so hard
There was nothing left
Over except a palm's worth
Of gold dust glinting in this
Smash of sunlight
So specific to the Midwest,
A day like this, that is,
When everything has happened

So many times already.
I see you, Finn, deep in mind,
Glowing at your edges
Like the astral I don't
Know what else did I not
Know about you besides
Everything, but I am certain
Your Mum & sister
Are emptied out no matter
How prepared they've been
In withdrawal from you
For so long
They shake
So violently
They appear still.
When I look out
The mirror to see
The world. When I
Flaw, abstractly, but
Precisely, like ice floes
Disappearing somewhere
North of here.
This place is jumping.
This place is all I can handle.
You people,
The fiction of our time
Lives inside this rhyme.
I can craft images that will
Make you an addict.
The rinse of dawn light
Reveals a half-built
Stadium claimed as domain

By roving lions. This
Apocalypse of potential
Futures, like Twin Earth
Parallel play, it's all
About how the self—which
We know is only
A Ponzi scheme, con-
Structed by quiet hacks
Quills in hand, blood
On the paper, blood
On the lips. How the self
Mutilating part of me
Just wants to rest
My feet after walking
Barefoot across the hot coals
Of poetry. & so, poetry,
Quite undetermined whether today
Is the day before yesterday, or
The day after tomorrow,
Or the week after next,
Fades away;
Andy & Fred & Finn fade away;
& Twemlow fades away;
& the stony self goes away—
Declines to fade, proving
Rock to the last—& even
The unknowns
Are slowly strained off,
& it is all over.

Responding to my father's question

I've described it as
"A silence as white
As hospital clouds."
I've tended to think
Of it as akin to
Occupying space,
Which is not like
Taking up space,
Which implies volition.
As you know,
I sat on a bench
In the mall, while
My friends were passing
Time in class.
High & thus utterly
Imprecise. Moments
Before I sat on the bench,
I had leafed through
The several copies of
The latest issue of *Details*
At the magazine kiosk
Because Dale had tipped
Us that there was an insert
In it that you could rip
From its perforation
& redeem anywhere
For a free pack of
True cigarettes. I
Unperfed six of them
& redeemed them

Immediately. I con-
Sidered this a non-
Trivial event. I
Destroyed this task.
How many ways
Can I tell you I
Killed time? You'd
Cringe to hear even
One story, its
Trace still
Tracking down
My spine,
Even now, twenty
Years later, like
Still doves.

Responding to my father's question

For instance, the day
We saw each other
For the first time
In a year, outside
Steve's apartment.
You somehow
Had somehowed
Your way to me.
I must've eaten
Ten clocks
Waiting for you
That day. I recall
Your seersucker
Suit waltzing
Toward me
In the crippling
Heat. You looked
Like a death
Sentence.
I wanted to expire
In every way possible.
Upon seeing you.
I had just woken up
From a night spent
Talking to a vending
Machine about Genet's
The Thief's Journal,
Which seemed as good
As any book at illustrating
How pointless. This

Was around the time
You later shredded all
The documents in which
You laid your claims
On me. Every interface
Was a fight to be won
Or lost. Every flower
Buds, & with that
Budding, Rorschach.
Tell me what you see:
Chronic maximal;
Sea of Strychnine;
Lysergic blooming
Rainbow. The '70s
So terribly wasted.

Responding to my father's question

Dale sold cold chronic.
From his apartment
A few blocks from
My crisis, which was
Ongoing & on mute.
Mike walked into that
Building not like he
Owned it. It owned
Him, but I couldn't
Exactly say that to
Anyone who
Might be occupying
The backseat with me.
They'd look at me
Funny & shoot
My face off. Which
Is all I ever hoped
For a. For a
Better reason to
Refuse the memory,
For example, though
I remember it in real
Time, cutting class
Driving to Mike's
House or Dale's apt.
Or BJ's mom's place
Or Kendra's mom was
Out of town so the day
Would be spent huffing
& touching each other

In ways that felt like
My first baptism. Arriving
At so many places
All at once, the faces
Happy & destroyed
& the one
Thing that held them
Together was the
Memory of money.
Which was not a
Memory. It was a day-
Dream. It looked like
Their parents asking
Me why their son or
Daughter Vesuvius.

Responding to my father's question

Within the driving
Back & forth, terrible
Dream on the couch,
Pacing through scenario
In which she comes
Back to me, but when
We agree to meet
At Edgewood park at a very
Specific time, she doesn't
Show, my dream says,
& I play it over & over
Like the dream requires.
I don't mean to be so
Opaque. I absolutely
Hated high school.
Mr. C. measuring
The distance between
The open window
Bottom & the ledge,
The Plexiglas spritz
He showered down
On each chair between
Classes. So high coming
Back to his class one day,
Investing myself back into
My chair, laughing a reverb
Repercussion into
Years of washing it off
My skin.
Shelly asked for

Some burrito, Lance
Hankered for permission
To unleash his very
Personal hounds.
What I'm trying to say
Is, Mr. C. stamped a lot
Of red ink across my
Interpretations of *Gatsby*.
Future Imperfect FAIL.
Passive Voice
FAIL.
I will have been I
Will have known
I shall be the object
Relation totally collapsing.

Responding to my father's question

A pillow of dust
To enshrine your legions
Of hallowed halls
Of your worth.
I keep expecting words
To do their work.
Your jowls
Hidden by the beard
You've worn my
Whole life, so I have no idea
What I'll look like after
You're dead. This beard
You told me years ago
That you could never
Shave as your patients
Wouldn't recognize
Themselves. I'm easy
Peasy as I fall to
Pieces. A choir of
Unrelenting dogs
Making meat of me.
I drove my truck
Into the guardrail
At 90 to test
The air bag. It
Worked out
For the both of us.
I'm a peddler
Of one-liners
In line at the food

Bank to check my
Credit line. All
The garlic bulbs I've
Been hoarding have
Grown beards. That's
A night's work knifing.
When you told me
You were pretty
Sure you were going
To hell, I told you
Wallace Stevens
Repented
On his so-called death-
Bed. Who the fuck
Is watching the TV.

Responding to my father's question

That's the third person
To message me.

You can't be serious.

You can't be serious.

You can't be serious.

You can't be serious.
Actually, I made that up.
He may as well have
Hydroplaned into a column
Of numbers binary-like &
Deified. You therapy
Much? You drain
The main vein? Open
It with a salve of serrated
Edges. A roomful of
Razor-sharp teeth chattering
The local nonsense, which
Keeps us all up at ungodly
Hours. I stabbed my pound
Of lasagna in its heart as
You sank into your
Inner zombie. We aren't
Going to get along
For much longer
If you keep bleeding from
Your inner eye like this.
All sorts of pathologies
Drain into you, out
Of you. You want to know

Why you can't stab a
Christmas tree into
The corner of my living
Room every Christmas
Holiday on repeat?
You have a Jewish
Grandson. It's that simple.
His name is the verb
We both swab our cankers
With. His name erupts
Cancerous & decorous,
Decorous & Camaro memories.

Responding to my father's question

I square dark spaces
In the places where
I'm an addict. I rinse &
Delete on repeat.
The addict
In me charms the
Awful offal, where
The memories (of you) collide
In stride, the memories
Of you glitch through.
Like tiny flashbacks
Flashing back your priors.
Now you tell me.
You think you're going
To hell. I look forward
To your review of the place.
The mild discomfort you'll
Feel is my two year old
Self wondering why
Mum looks so
Peaked & wearing
Hospital gown. She could
Barely look at me the one
Visit I remember taking.
There was an inner
Courtyard teeming with
Plants. She seemed to prefer
Being in there than being
Anywhere else. If you feel
Anything for her. If you

Can't stand all the
Involuntary
Redress. You've spent
Most of your life
Listening to the berserk
Among us spit our
Holiness at you. That'd
Kill most of you, which
It did. I can't come this
Weekend. I'm grilling
For three these days.
As my friend said when
She was pregnant with
Her only child, at brunch,
"Bacon wants sausage."

Responding to my father's question

I'm rolling on the floor
In my humble.
For what it's,
In my humble.
If I recall
On the other.
All this etcetera
Seeping into my tapped
Veins. All this
Life being reviewed.
You picked me up
From Mum's one day
In a question delivered
As a strike to my chakras.
"Steak and peas,"
I answered. You knew
I'd been eating ham
Sandwiches every night
For years. You asked
To cover your. It feels
Good, don't it. It's not
Like you had your wife
Serve me steak that night.
The mild embarrassment
Of being alive swarmed
Us. I still can't wrap
My head. I lived in
Two tax codes. My fifty
Closest neighbors didn't
Know to college. As your

Fourth child, I'm supposed
To be the dumbest. I
Dumb & gum up
The rips & tears.
I once lit a black cat
Firecracker in hand
& it short fused
A reverb straight through
Me. Thought I lost
My hand. Wished I
Had. Not for local
Camera love, just
Wanted to feel something
Despair into you within
Kaleidoscopic tropics.

Responding to my father's question

Verily I believe these
Trees sway with &
Against the winds.
Wishing you were
Here with me,
Dialing the tiny blips
Registering across
Cosmos: aslant:
Au courant. There's
An app for the absence
You wade into/out of
All day: a map of
Your interiority, which
Flames apart infernal &
Reckoning. These diurnal
Abysses full of missed
Reminiscences. I've been
A mange of static in these
Poems these trees. Some
Poems some trees some
Thing alights on something.
I used a lot of time as a kid
Fraying myself into the kind
Of person I'd been told
I'd hate to become. By this
I mean I spent all my free
Time thinking about the con-
Sequence of you. When I
Teach my students
The basics of narrative

Filmmaking, at some point
I have to talk about sequences.
Which are series of shots
Strung together to convey
Some part of the narrative.
Any sequence is as arbitrary
As a tornado touching down.
You remind me of the Zeus
Who cannot live with
Himself & so impales
Himself on a mountaintop.
Where do we go from
Here it's all small talk.
How's the whether
We care or knot.

Responding to my father's question

These are my last thoughts.
They decompose as I write
Them they are a kind of recompense.
I've established something:
Wide shot of sailors breaking
Down at horizon
Snapping into a velvety seam.
I had wished for such a brighter
Past for you to forage, but
I had forgotten you'd forget
Any of this. My
Opacity like the steady drip
Of fentanyl fanning (flushing) through
Me as the doctor summons
His gods & takes a knee.
I wish I could [insert here].
I'd be spent cartridge
Smoking. A diamond
In the skyward phase
The sun streaking
Its greasy fingers across
Something. Something
Finer, something perhaps
Resigned to its. An a cappella
Rendering of S. painting
Pocked canvasses. Ghosted
Fish thrashing. Colossal French
Doors smashing. Verily, it's
Static stitching past lives
Into a parlor trick. James

Meant what he said. He
Needed you to put your hand
On his back & recall
Him back into his life. I've
Probably never loved anyone
As much as I did him
Back then, which was an
Astronaut's life cycle.
Prince dies. James doesn't
Call. I kicked a kid
In the stomach because
I'm a relatively bad example
Of Telemachus unhinging in
The corner office of your
Inclination. Get me the fuck-
Ing music hates me. Ablate
The beat goes on with or
Without you. Ablate I'm
Late ablate I'm late ablate

Attributed to the Harrow Painter

When I was twelve,
My tennis coach asked me
To pose for him after practice.
I'm an artist, he told me,
I coach to pay the bills.
He loved Greek vase work.
Largely, he said while
Inching his thumb
Just under the lip
Of my underwear,
Because pottery
Is pretty much all we know
Of Greek painting.
It's all that's survived.
He had an easel
In his office, his kit, a stool
To sit on. He knew every
Angle of light
In that locker room,
All of it bronze & loamy
In my memories, steam
Flowering from the wet
Concrete underfoot.
I don't know why I stood
For him so many times.
He showed me pictures.
He talked while he worked.
His worldview, he
Acknowledged, was mediated
By his reading of

The charcoal sketch I made
Of Lennon & Ono's
Rolling Stone cover,
Where they lie
In state,
Seething with hate
In my rendering,
Slotted with guilt &
Rotting from the
Outside in.
The whole thing
Was a riot,
A ball, I've dined out
On my recollections
Of what became
Our weekly sessions,
For years. Whatever
I know I owe him.
Of course this isn't
True, but the meme
Persists. I can't look
At anything in a museum
Without thinking about him.
Our lessons migrated
From the locker room
To his flat,
Which was larded
With shelves
Of expensive art
Books hemmed in
By a fifteenth-century settee
Once owned by

A Vanderbilt,
The guilt he must've
Felt spreading his legs
On that thing,
Reaching . . .
In my memories,
Everything is in
Hushed tones.
He shrugged through
A phalanx of streaked
Glasses of cheap sherry
(He showed me—
Once I busted through
Puberty—how I could
Continue my education
During my morning shave.
He had me stand back & to the left
Of him in his tiny bathroom
As he lathered his face
With his buttery shaving cream
& held his half-read copy
Of whatever Durrell-brother
Novel he was savoring.
He flipped pages with his
Left pointer finger as he
Picked up the straight razor
His father had left him
With his right hand
& carefully shaved
His whitening stubble.)
He continued to paint
Me, I continued to

Pretend I was attuned
To chiaroscuro, at least
How Renaissance Italians
Reckoned with & employed
It, ghastly noirs
Filmed before the moving
Image was possible.
I became a mentee
& I became too much
To bear,
Everyone I knew
Kept asking me
If I was carrying
Their burdens like
I said I would,
I said I would.
You could find me
Most days dead happy,
Slouched next to
A strobe light,
Mainlining its perilous
Flashing queries into
My face, my face
Eating light like time
Does this frayed life.
& Andy would
Check in on me
& James told me
He'd be back in five
& Hudson chased
After so many fireflies
He reached for his cell

To dial 911 &
Realized this was 1991
& all he grabbed
Was air. Lance? Zoble?
Rooney? Fro? This is
What I mean.
A series of queries
Better left unheeded.
I hate, a phrase I've
Banished from the house
I call my own as
I owned
The truck
I stole
To ride out
The gaps between
Waking up & frying
Out, I sat
In the cab
In my high school
Parking lot as class
Passed time as I
Passed time
As time passed
Time, it was skull-
Fuck cold.
As I smoked
& stared out between
The slashes of frost
On the window,
Not thinking
So much as enduring

This adolescence
Became a lesson
In how to wait
For nothing to happen.
He asked me
To read Kenneth
Clark's *Civilisation*
I don't know
How many times.
Every time I see
That book I retch,
Which happened
Recently at a dinner
Party (He taught me
How, as host,
To be the last
To lift my fork
To my open mouth).
I spotted a copy
Of that fucking
Book. What else
Can be said that hasn't
Already been &
Much worse &
Awfully & all of this
Sounds like I
Am not attuned
To the pleasures
I've been afforded.
True.
He asked too
Much of me.

I later understood.
I don't know why I stood
For him so many times.
You can't always have
What you won't
Do to get a piece of me.
My big takeaway
Was that there are certain
Texts—these can be poems,
Novels & essays, also
Paintings, sculptures,
Even operas—
You internalize. Sometimes,
You read the wrong thing
At the wrong time
& poof! There it goes
All getting under your skin
For life!
Kundera's *The Un-*
Bearable Lightness of Being
Absolutely destroyed me.
I read it at the most perfectly
Wrong time. I was fifteen
& dropping
Out of school & acid
& there you go, a novel
About an emasculated intellectual
Who turns to sex to
Make sense of his new reality
As a window washer.
Kundera licked his lips
After chowing down

On some Memphis BBQ,
Or, rather, the prospect
Of redressing old wounds
In the presence of a woman
Naked, save for a hat.
A novel that chronicles
How a man is always
The sum of his conquests.
History of literature in one
Word: don't be silly,
It takes four:
Take off your clothes.
What we have on record
Is a script under constant
Revision, redlined &
Augmented by our comrades
In mellifluous arms.
Our poets, who grow soft
& perish at the thought.
(I am one of them)
(I've been writing
This poem for a decade
& each draft continues
To remind me how
Removed I am from
Everything: I've no gloss
I can offer you. I lost
My keys somehow
In the snow yesterday
My son, my son . . .)
I recognize now
A hole in my thinking

A hole into which
I think,
A world
Happening passing
Faster than
The link
To this time lapse
I found in a forum
Dedicated to discussion
Of the phenomenon
Of artists who are born
& die on the same day,
So ephemeral their
Medium. Most of
The users in the forum
Had resigned themselves
To documenting
Their own oblivion,
But they were dedicated. This was home. This was family.
This forum,
Which is shabby & decayed
Not by time but
An ancient
Handsomeness
—*Kalos* is the Greek word
For it—massed
All these millennia—
I'm being sloppy,
Kalos means all kinds
Of things, the Harrow Painter
Was too sloppy
To put too fine a point

On it—
Seen from this distance—
Like intergalactic light,
So incredibly old
By the time we see it
Every possible god
Is not dust but
Nothing, once a part
Then none, not unlike
The pleasure I used
To take in reading
In bed as a child,
A refuge from
Whatever disaster
At hand, not thinking
Then how years later
I would write coverage
Of screenplays
For a small production co.
In New York,
& during this time
I learned to hate
Reading anything
That was for sale.
Eventually we'll all
Write a screenplay
That moves with speed &
Aplomb & whom
Would you cast
As your mother?
I gave my second-grade teacher
A reason to retire

Upon presenting to class this
History of Greece.
I showed a time-lapse
Video of a slug's
Slime trail. It begins
In earnest.
A slug full of hope,
Hungry for knowledge
Of where its next
Meal would come from.
A few glasses of sherry
Later, the trail looks like
Kyle Lambert's finger painted
Re-creation
Of a photo of
Morgan Freeman,
The creation of which
You can watch in time-lapse
Here: http://www.kylelambert.co.uk/gallery/morgan-freeman/
This feels like the end,
I thought to myself
After I watched this
After searching for
"Famous finger-painting artists"—
Was trying to locate
The primitive artist
Savvy enough
To begin his/her career
As *primitive*.
What's interesting is that
The poet Jack Gilbert used to watch
The poet Jack Spicer play pinball.

Jack Gilbert lived on
The Greek island of Santorini,
Where pinball sleeps
In the cycloptic eye of time.
Jack Gilbert Graham, not
A poet as far as I know,
Killed forty-four people
By planting a dynamite bomb
Onboard
A United Airlines Douglas DC-6B
Departing from
Denver, Colorado,
On November 1, 1955.
His mother
Kept her head down
Upon takeoff,
Counting the diamond
Shapes dilating in her hose.
Jack Gilbert Graham took out
$37,500 worth of life insurance
On his mother
In the airport,
From a vending machine,
Just before takeoff.
He was gassed
In a Colorado prison
Less than two years later.
The flight was bound
For Portland, Oregon,
Where in March of 2003 I picked up
The poet
Jack Gilbert

To drive him to Eugene
For a reading.
For two hours, he asked me
What it was like
Living in New York
During the dot-com boom.
He wanted to know what
The sex was like,
His enthusiasm,
He admitted,
Was the last thing
He wanted to lose.
When he read
That night, he repeated
A poem
He had read earlier
In the evening.
He realized this
After he finished it,
Said it was a poem
He really liked so
He wanted to hear it again.
I imagine
Greece is a nice place
If you're Zeus
& you rape
The peasants & livestock
So often
You need a second cock.
It's true. It's in Ovid.
Look, I've loved my mother
Most of my life.

I'm a decent neighbor
In that I don't care
What my neighbors
Are up to, like
I don't pick up the phone
When Jim sits on his back porch
All night yelling at his phone
Fisting a bottle of Jack Daniels.
That's his choice,
Even if it keeps Sacha
Up hours that all of us
Lose forever. I'm a humanist,
After all. I respect
Your desire to pour
Everything into
A poem. When
Jack Gilbert
Died, I hadn't thought
Of him
For a decade.
I barely knew him
Except what he
Showed me in his poems,
Little fists of light
Illuminating the
Rock path he'd
Pace night
After night,
Pulling his famous
White beard
Into focus
As he fixed

His gaze
Onto the poor
Creatures
Littering his view,
Leaving his readers
To bronze his poems—
These well-wrought
Urns (all they do is
Burn you out)—while
Those poor creatures
Continue to pick
Through the trash,
Every day returning
To the same heap
To bend at the waist
To sort through,
To discover
Something to bring
Home to put on the table
To bolt down so as
To not taste
To not remember
That tomorrow
Another long walk
To the same heap.
They will be recast
As quotidian miracles,
Abstracted into evidence
That we must
Press on, push through
Our suffering
Into our pleasure,

Or we are defeated.
& we, the readers,
Should be
Indebted to him
For looking their way
& taking his time
To chisel them into words?
I don't know
If it matters
What a poet
Was like in
Real life. Some say
You just read the poems
Sans biography.
Others are obsessed
With ethics.
Do you try to glean
A life from a
Collection of poems?
Is the reader supposed
To identify with
A poem anymore?
Are we, to paraphrase
Nabokov, to maze
Through a great
Text having left
Our own desire
To find ourselves
In it at the door,
As it were?
The great poem
Is chiseled rock.

The great poem
Rages with
White fire.
The great poem
Vomits in the
Restaurant bathroom
After a spiteful
Dinner with an ex.
The great poem
Steals rolls
Of toilet paper
Every chance it gets.
The great poem
Is always at risk,
Underfunded,
Destitute, on the dole,
Full of shame,
Paroled, poorly
Invested, scabrous.
I want to end this
Poem rich with shame—
The sunflower
Hacked at its stem,
Fibers shredded across
The ground, an icy wind
Brisks in the vatic
Shame I came here
To tell you about.
That this man,
Who took me to
My first (& only)
Chamber opera

When I was seventeen
& versed in the pain
Of endurance, died
Two years ago,
Leaving behind
A first-rate collection
Of books that he had
Left to me years
Before when he asked
Me to be sole beneficiary
& executor of
His will, well, things
Happen in the gaps.
He made an awful
Remark to my stepmother
Over lunch a few months
Before my wedding,
It was both what he called
My future wife & how
He put it, spitting out
The word, I don't
Want to repeat it
Anymore, it has taken on
Its own blemished lore.
That was the end
Of it all. He asked me
To read *Civilisation*
& I declined.

NOTE

A note on the Harrow Painter, from Michael Padgett's article, "The Harrow Painter, with a Note on the Geras Painter":

The Harrow Painter was named by J. D. Beazley [in a 1916 *JHS* article titled "Two Vases in Harrow"] after an oino-choe at Harrow school with a picture of a handsome boy holding a hoop. Along with the Kleophrades Painter, the artist was the subject of one of Beazley's earliest articles, in which he attributed 39 vases to this "minor" pot-painter, whom he later called "a poorly-equipped painter whose ordinary employment was daubing cheap neck-amphorae and column-kraters with dull and ill-drawn forms." These are harsh words, though not wholly inaccurate, for although he has been justly called "more than ordinarily competent," the Harrow Painter was indeed a minor talent, not withstanding the undeniable charm of some of his works. If, however, one looks beyond the quality of his line and his relatively low standing in the artistic panthe-on, one discovers in him many elements of interest and more than a few delightful pictures.

ACKNOWLEDGMENTS

....

"Looking at Schnabel's *The Death of Fashion* with my son"
appeared in *Lana Turner*. "The speaker's feeling of loneli-
ness is profound, or I read the lyrics of the emergency"
appeared in *The Literary Review*. "Champagne Dawn"
appeared in *jubilat*. "I wanted to write you a love poem"
appeared in *Court Green*. "Attributed to the Harrow Paint-
er" appeared in *The Paris Review*. A section of "Burnett's
Mound" appeared in the *Coe Review* under the title "He
was everything to me, for a brief, blazing time in my life."
Thanks to the editors.

KUHL HOUSE POETS

Christopher Bolin
Ascension Theory

Shane Book
Congotronic

Oni Buchanan
Must a Violence

Michele Glazer
On Tact, & the Made Up World

David Micah Greenberg
Planned Solstice

Jeff Griffin
Lost and

John Isles
Ark

John Isles
Inverse Sky

Aaron McCollough
Rank

Randall Potts
Trickster

Bin Ramke
Airs, Waters, Places

Bin Ramke
Matter

Michelle Robinson
The Life of a Hunter

Vanessa Roveto
bodys

Robyn Schiff
Revolver

Robyn Schiff
Worth

Sarah V. Schweig
Take Nothing with You

Rod Smith
Deed

Cole Swensen
The Book of a Hundred Hands

Cole Swensen
Such Rich Hour

Tony Tost
Complex Sleep

Pimone Triplett
Supply Chain

Nick Twemlow
Attributed to the Harrow Painter

Susan Wheeler
Meme

Emily Wilson
The Keep